BOOK 1

Grand Duets for Piano

8 EARLY ELEMENTARY PIECES FOR ONE PIANO, FOUR HANDS

Melody Bober

I can still remember performing my very first piano duet. The sound of four hands playing together was amazing. Whether playing with my teacher or a friend, it was always exciting to make music together.

While duets are enjoyable, they also offer a great musical experience for students. Rhythm, phrasing, articulation and dynamics all become wonderful teaching tools while students learn to listen for that unique blending of parts. I have written *Grand Duets for Piano*, Book 1, so that today's piano students can have as much fun as I did. The duets in this collection contain music in a variety of keys, styles, meters and tempos designed to help students progress technically and musically...together!

Duets continue to spark excitement in my studio. I sincerely hope that you will enjoy these *Grand Duets for Piano*!

Best wishes,

CONTENTS

Copyright © MMIX by Alfred Publishing Co., Inc.
All rights reserved.   Printed in USA.
ISBN-10: 0-7390-5899-1
ISBN-13: 978-0-7390-5899-2

Alfred

Twilight Tune

Secondo

Melody Bober

Delicately (♩ = 92)
(Both hands one octave lower throughout)

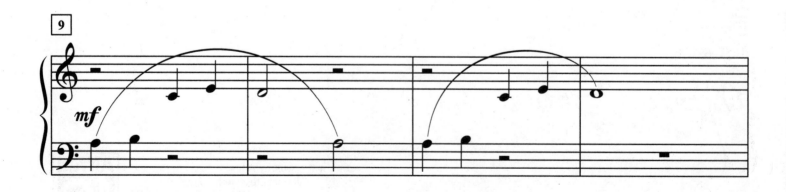

Twilight Tune

Primo

Melody Bober

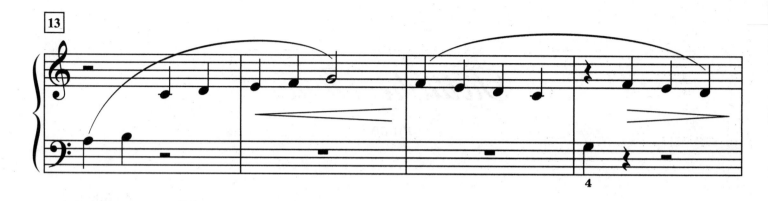

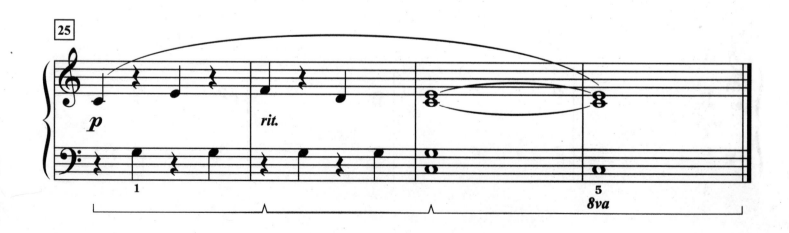

Hot Popcorn!

Secondo

Melody Bober

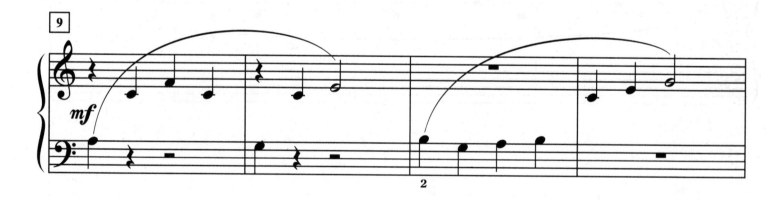

Hot Popcorn!

Primo

Melody Bober

Lively (♩ = 160)
(Both hands one octave higher throughout)

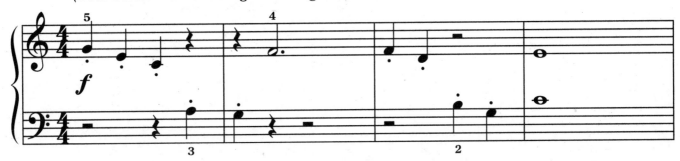

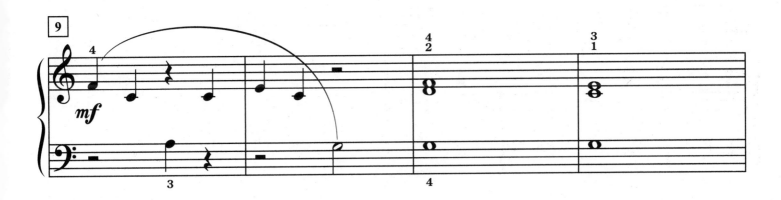

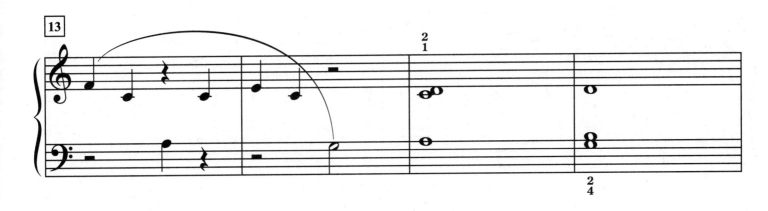

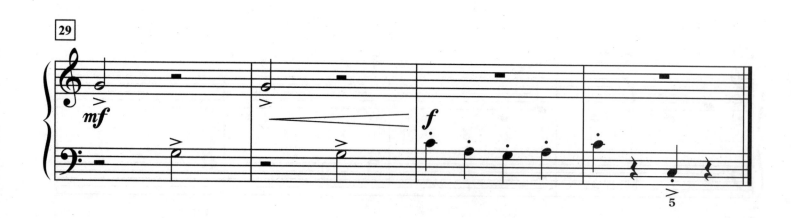

Back and Forth Waltz

Secondo

Melody Bober

Gracefully ($\bullet$ = 144–152)
(Both hands one octave lower throughout)

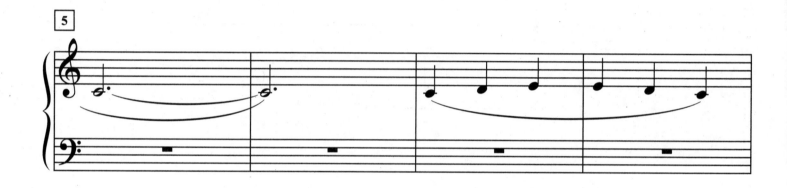

Back and Forth Waltz

Primo

Melody Bober

Gracefully (♩ = 144–152)
(Both hands one octave higher throughout)

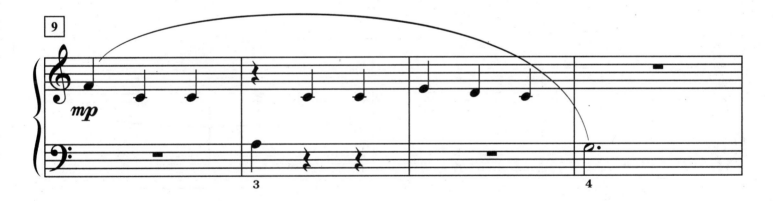

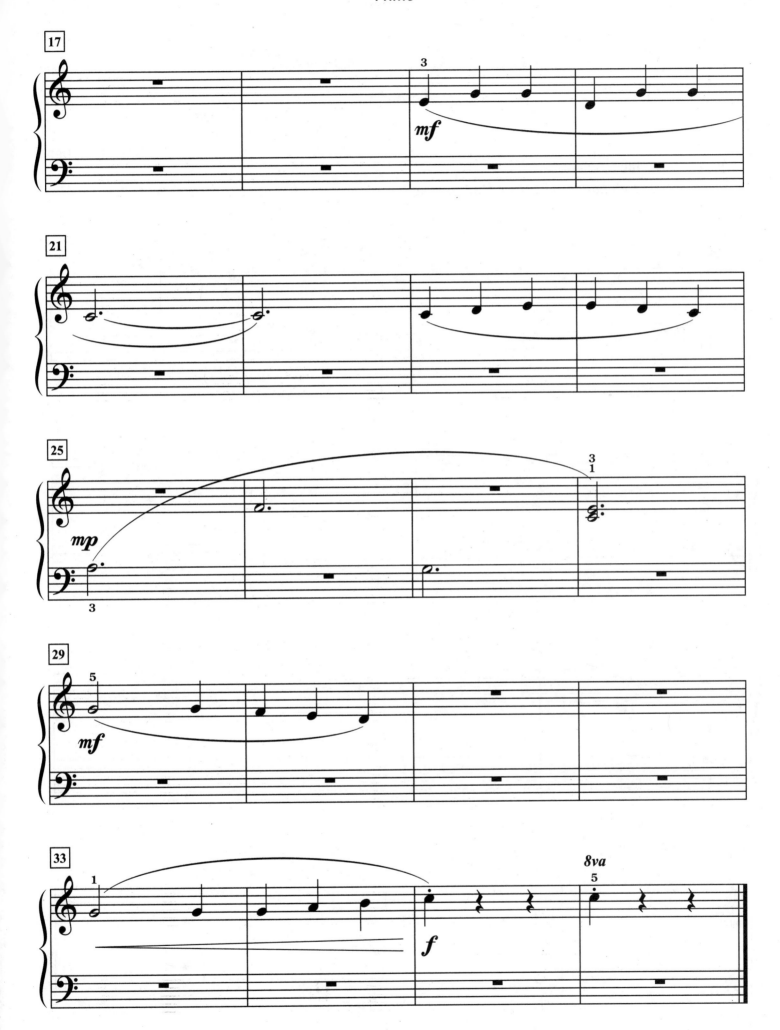

Race Car Boogie

Secondo

Melody Bober

Racing ($\half = 84$–88)
(Both hands one octave lower throughout)

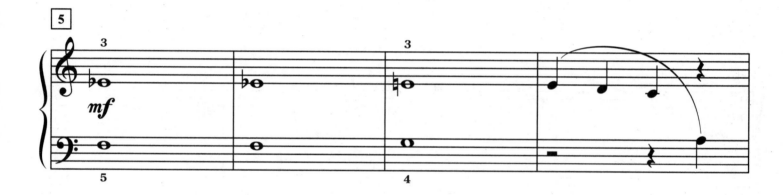

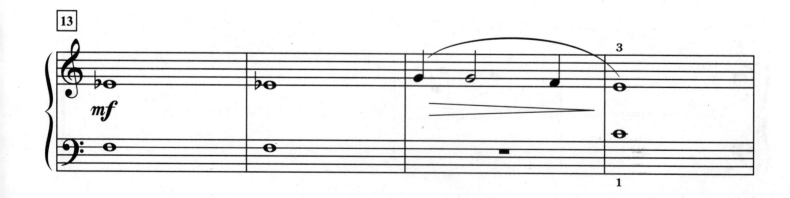

Race Car Boogie

Primo

Melody Bober

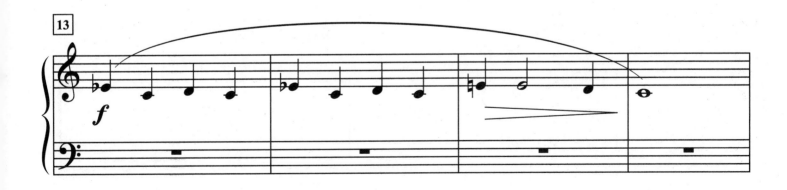

Listen to the Wind

Secondo

Melody Bober

Flowing ($\d = 72$)
(Both hands one octave lower throughout)

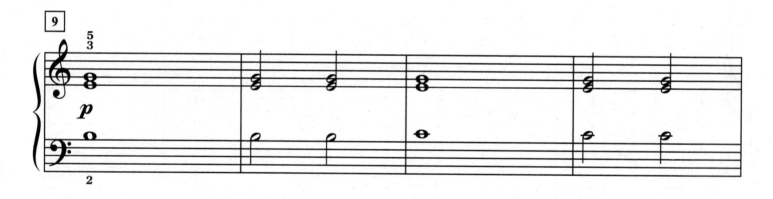

Listen to the Wind

Primo

Melody Bober

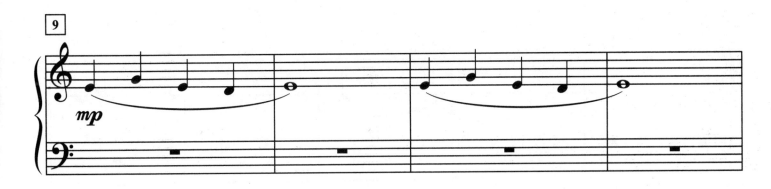

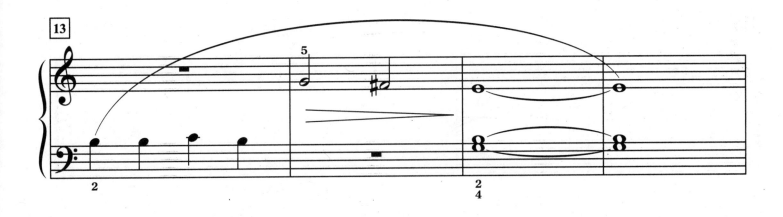

A Mysterious Adventure

Secondo

Melody Bober

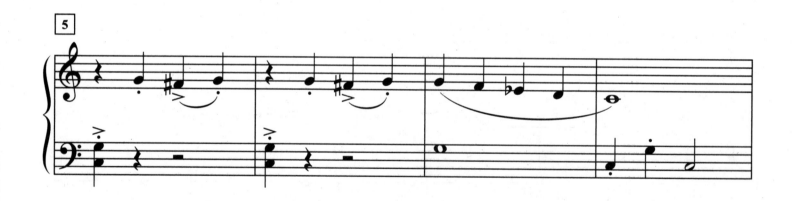

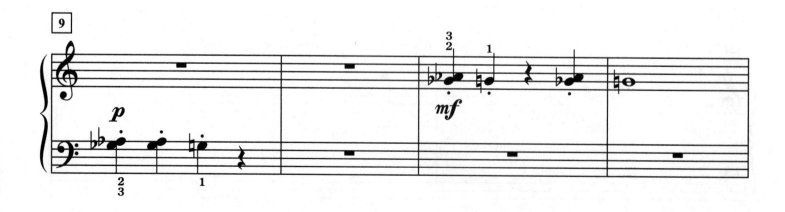

A Mysterious Adventure

Primo

Melody Bober

Mysteriously (♩ = 132–138)
(Both hands one octave higher throughout)

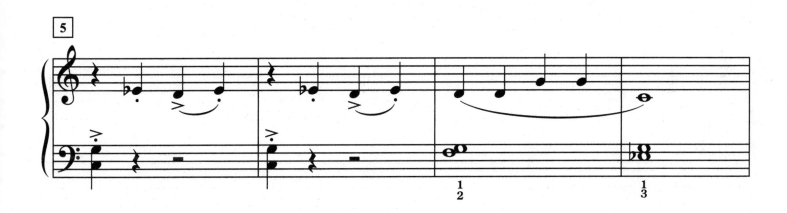

13

17

21

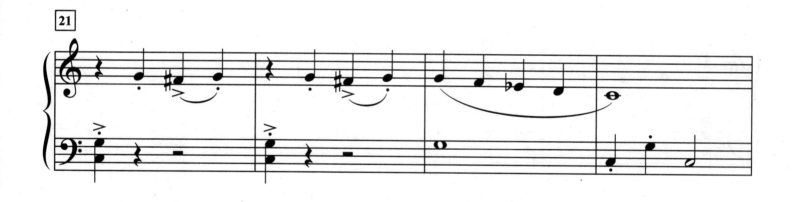

25

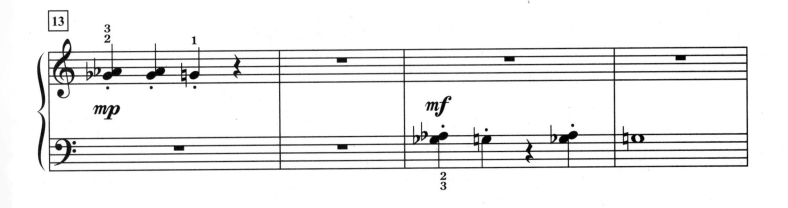

Hometown Celebration

Secondo

Melody Bober

Briskly (♩ = 80)
(Both hands one octave lower throughout)

Hometown Celebration

Primo

Melody Bober

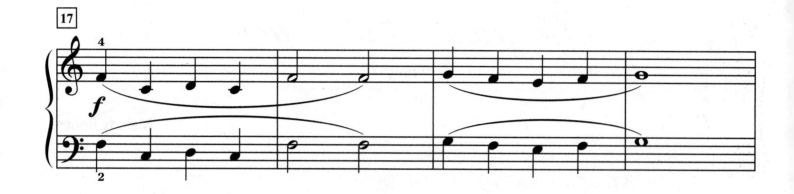

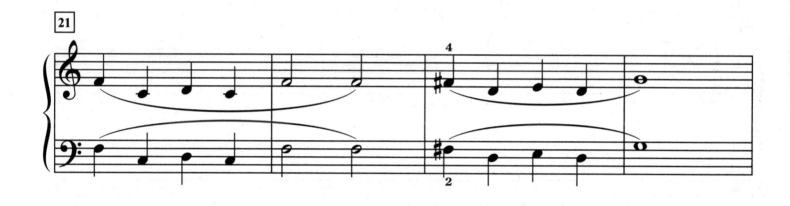

Dance Class

Secondo

Melody Bober

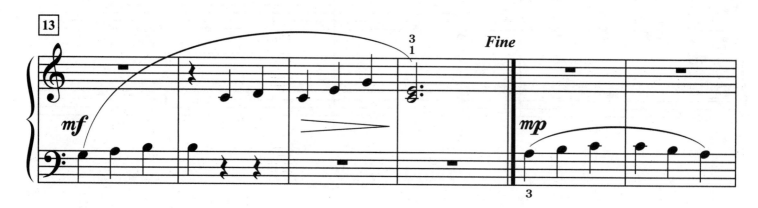

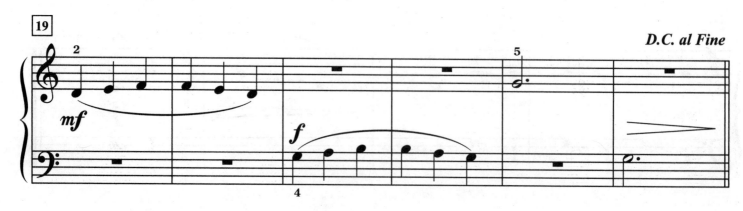

Dance Class

Primo

Melody Bober

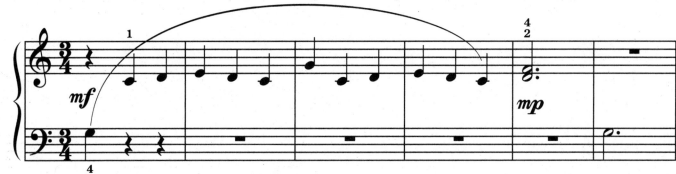

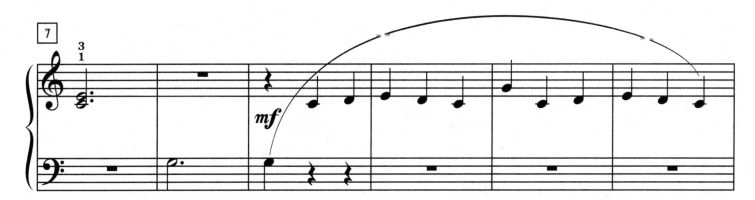

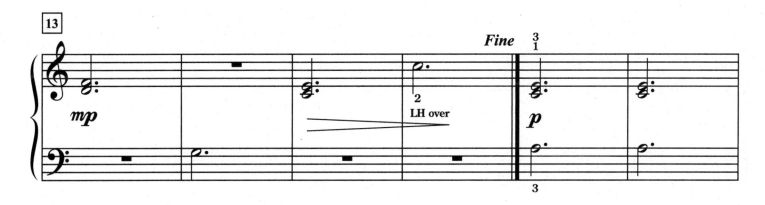

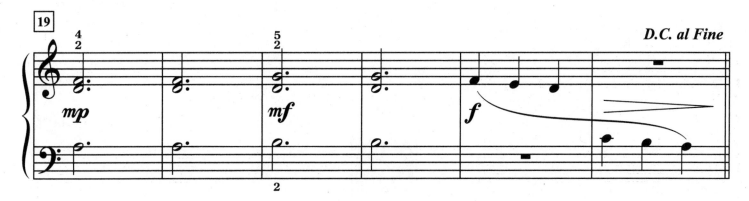